Hi,
My Name Is Sally
i first dropped from a cloud
To My Mommy And Daddy.
Then in 1981 my life complete
24 years later when Heaven Allowed
True Love Came So Sweet.
I dreamed of the day
since i was a wee tyke
Then Magic Came My Way
i found out what paradise was like.
(and the rest is history* * * *
Copyright 2012
And He Inspired The Poetry In....
(Sally) That's Me
Little did i know
when i'd grow
the poetry would just flow!!!!

thee angels cried

© s@L 2001

Dear World:
I am disheartened by the way-
you worship (things)! And forsake thy neighbor.
There are people starving,
there are people dying !
Take time to help a friend in need,
take time to help a stranger !
Love your things, BUT
DON'T worship them-PLEASE !
Human life is precious,
i put it here FOR YOU.
I gave you the world, so that you
could learn-not every wish comes true !
I'm sorry for the hardships,
i'm sorry for the pain.
BUT learn from these and be better
don't live your life in vain !
I know that things can't hurt you,
and sometimes people do !
Try to overcome the bad, and
LET THE GOOD SHINE THRU !
    i love you, GOD

this 1 started it all....

Nice Nice Baby............
Alright stop what you're doin and listen,
you make me shine and glisten.
Turn off the lights and watch me glow to the beat,
from my head down to my feet.
To the extreme i steal your time like a vandal,
light up my face like a candle.
Dance the night away in all the rooms,
you got me smokin can't ya smell the fumes?!
Better call in an arson cop,
cause this fire just won't stop.
Love just radiates from me,
cause you perform it so magically.
Your power holds me tightly,
i sing like a bird daily and nightly.
Killing me softly with your sweet melody,
anything less would be a tragedy.
Yo VIP you just don't quit,
when i got a problem you kick it.
Take heed i'm a rappin fool,
you taught me things not learned in school.
Your style's like a chemical spill,
you got it flowin can't get my fill.
Nice Nice Baby........
by Cherry Ice And The Candles............
aka~S@L~
Copyright 2010

The little girl was so happy and loved. Everybody thought she was just the cutest thing.

But sometimes she got sad and would(do) the cutest thing. She would rub the satin trim on her blanket and say gike gike gike.

Her Mommy
Dressed Her Up So Cute,
in outfits she made taboot!

~~1 satiny~~ comfort 2011 from heaven

When i was just a wee lass,
i had a comfort zone.
But it was not my blanket,
for my gikey was all my own.
I'd suck my thumb,
while rubbing the satin trim.
And say gike-gike-gike
away my blues went on a whim.
When i became a big lass,
still at times i felt blue.
I took comfort in knowing that,
with the love of my life beside me:
there's nothing i couldn't get thru.
Without him now to touch:
there's no comfort to cling to!.
My comforting Pooh Bear
Is In My Heart 4ever there.........
but to not be able to touch him just isn't fair!
Copyright 2011
Sally

and her name is,Tinymite

I see how cold the world can be,
before I'm even born.
I ask the Lord to keep me,
where I'll be safe and warm.
There is so much good that is hardly shown,
if I could I'd make it better when I'm grown.
A nice lady keeps me protected
in her tummy,
her love is ever so kind.
I never see darkness inside my Mommy,
for only shelter I can find.
I'm just a wee tyke: nobody hears my plea,
i cry so when seeing hate and the like:
is anybody listening to me?!
Stop the racket i'm trying to sleep in here,
i'm not ready to face the world yet:
and i'm trembling with fear!
Please don't bring me into
such a scary place,
would it hurt you to love one another
and bring a smile to my tiny face?!
I see in the future
a new world coming:
with a boy named faron 2be with 4ever!!
My Mommy kept me safe until the day
My Special Angel Faron came my way!!
Copyright 2011
Sally

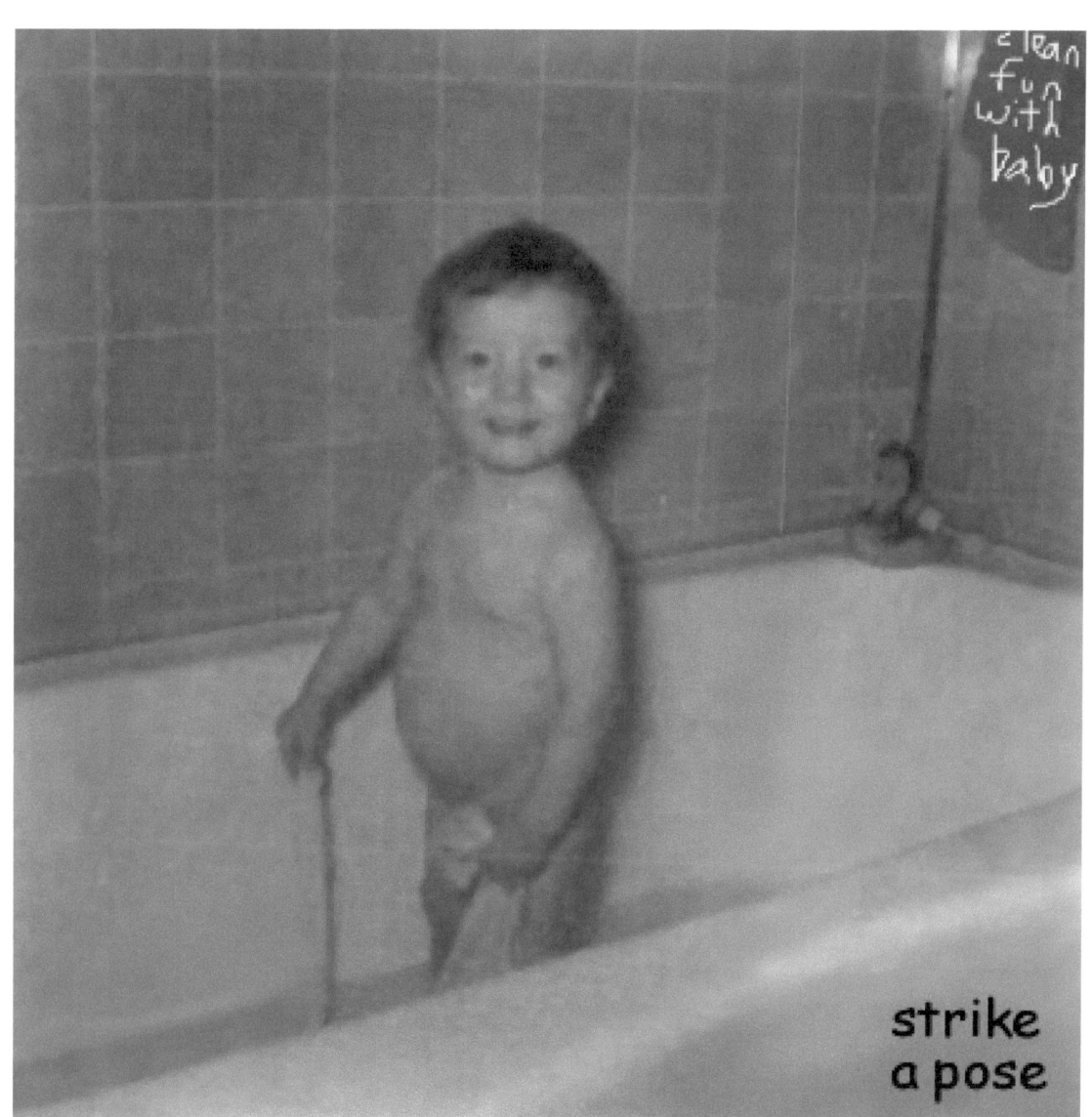

 This became known as her Gikey. Such Comfort!

the changing questions of a child

****
****
****
****
****
****
****
****
****
******************)
Mommy-why is the sky blue?
Daddy-who turns on the stars at night?
Mommy-where do babies come from?
Daddy-why are they shooting at you?
Mommy-why do people fight?
Daddy-why does bad come?
Mommy,Daddy-will the world ever
       get along just right?
And why was The Love Of My Life
taken without warning:
like a thief in the night?
Copyright 2010~S@L~(that was Me)
Revised Copyright 2012
Sally

Baby Love

If you can't love
with all you got why even try,
but it's hard to lose with
hearts&roses&sweets oh my.
Get down on your knees
and thank God above,
for sending you
a sugar baby to love.
It matters not
if girl or boy,
just be thankful for
your even sweeter bundle of joy.
The rubette dancers
bless you from the start,
to see that love rocks
all over your heart.
I know cause my heart's still rockin
from the sweetest drop of sugar,
sent from heaven
and nothing could compare no sir!
Copyright 2010~S@L~

a babe thru the ages

They say we're old and about life we don't know,
we lost our minds a long time ago.
Well who's to say if that's true,
cause i forgot what i just said to you.
Babe my memory fades-
my memory fades.
They say it's been time well spent,
but there's time we don't know where it went.
Well our get up and go we've lost a lot
the fartherest we go now is the pot,
I'll Never Forget The Love We've Got.
Even Tho Babe my memory fades-
my memory fades.
I got ringing in my ears,
i see wrinkles in the mirrors.
And when i sleep out like a light,
it matters not if day or night.
So let them say i get confused,
cause i don't care at least i'm amused.
Then put his big hand in mine,
who cares if we're not in our prime.
Babe my memory fades-
my memory fades.
I got him my better half,
i got him to make me laugh.
I got him to talk with me,
i got him to limp with me.
I got him to pass the time,
i got him and he's all mine.
I got him i love so,
i got him even tho...............
My Memory Fades!
Copyright 2009~S@L~

Stay Young

Never take for granted
full of promise as a kid
all grown up now
you look back and how
the time has passed by
did you even try
to imagine
what a sin
the world would
lose such good
without the mind
of children and their kind
thinking innocently
how it should be
they're forced to
grow up so fast thru
life today
don't take childhood away
stay young at heart
let little things play a big part
like how your true love throws a fit
when his tickle he doesn't get!
Copyright 2012
Sally

such truth in much youth

The fastest way to a grown up's heart,
is a child at play
where innocence is a big part.
Children are so much like snowflakes,
each one different for goodness sakes.
Some are quiet as a mouse,
while others have run of the house.
They seem to be getting smarter,
must be something in the water.
The water i drank as a kid,
had fish diddle in it my daddy said it did.
It tickled as it went down,
it was some of the best times around.
Today everything is preserved too much,
it takes away that special touch.

In my day my talent was simple,
with just one look i could
charm the meanest soul.
I'm not saying kids shouldn't
be smart no way,
but let them be kids
childhood soon enuff goes away.
It shouldn't be a competition
on the block....
to see which one is
the first to talk.
Hold them in your hands and
marvel at the magic,
they are little drops of heaven
with pureness we seek.
And 1 grew up to be
MY SOULMATE THRU ETERNITY
Copyright 2012
Sally

Baby Still Wants

I want somebody
here to keep me company
i'm so lonely
nobody visits me
i'm in misery!
The misery won't end
cause i don't have my best friend
here my heart won't mend
but if someone would just spend
time w/me on that i could depend!
Nobody takes me anywhere
special or surprises me w/a momento here+there
if somebody would just care
that i've too much to bear
there's got to be enuff heart to spare!
I want my gikey
tho it's not enuff security
as My Honey
i wanna go back to being a baby
when i had not a pain or worry!
Copyright 2012
You're never too old to wanna hold
something to feel closely and warmly.
When i grew up Faron i was thankful to meet
the birdy didn't sing tweet tweet tweet
it sang gike gike gike from comfort so sweet....
Sally

the tale of a mermaid

Celebrate every second of every day,
you never know when they'll be taken away....

A woman to be in her prime
who had just lost her soul mate,
whom she knew
with the angels went to heaven:
couldn't grasp the idea and for her
birthday wish wanted to see him again.
She was at a local carnival
and wanted a balloon so,
she picked the mermaid
for she liked them so much.
She wondered if heaven
has a mailbox!
She decided to
write Her True Love a note and
tie it to the balloon.
She left it go and away it went
into the clouds where
a beam of light appeared.
Look everybody it's Faron
he found my balloon.
Thinking no more of it,
other than the sun glowing brightly
she had to leave.
A week later an envelope came in the mail.
It seems a man out hunting
came upon the balloon.
He took it home to his family,
not wanting to get her hopes up
but just couldn't ignore it.
It's plain to see tho;
Faron upon finding the balloon sent it to
these people so that his Sweetheart would know;
he hadn't forgot her or her birthday.
And what a gift-a miracle from
a mermaid from a town
across the horizon called mermaid!
(he also sent the angels along
 to sing her a song-My Special Angel
still to this day Heart And Soul)
Copyright 2012
Sally

beauty and the beast of burden

Leafing thru the day
as if to say,
i'm on my way
sorry i can't stay.
She came with beauty
for all to see,
golden slumber will be
bareness will come quickly.
Stripped of treasures bold
left in the cold,
where once was gold
with wonder to behold.
Given rarity not shaken
again she will awaken,
when she is taken
to heights not forsaken.
All of me believes
what my heart conceives,
magic never really leaves
thus spared by thieves.
One must stand tall
and dare not fall,
weather burdens and all
due time will call!
(THE STORY CONTINUES)
Copyright 2011
all in due time
cause he's rightfully mine....
Sally

11th Heaven Because He Was Here

On march eleven 2011
an angel went to heaven,
and Faron is his name
a miracle to me he came.
This date i needn't say
was the worst in every way,
except for the few moments we shared
that hug and kiss that Heaven spared.
That day i was in 11th heaven but such a short while
at least i got to see his smile,
and his wings flapped over me
then he flew away the worst tragedy.
Now of the day it's hard to speak
an end to my suffering i now seek,
every angel God could think of
carried him back to heaven above.
Twas march 11 of 2011 his last day on earth
i pray for our reunion with all i'm worth,
but i feel him here,
spiritually blessing everyone he gets near!
Copyright 2012
Sally

BABY COME BACK

Please Come Home
Please Come Home
I'm So Alone
I'm So Alone
Every Single Day I Cry
Every Single Day I Cry
Oh I Just Wanna Die
Oh I Just Wanna Die....
But i'm dead already
Dig a hole for my useless shell of a body
The room is spinning i'm so dizzy
I hope the gravediggers aren't too busy!
Happy Birthday Dear
Happy Birthday
Please God send him home here
he should be with me.
The Birthday Boy where is he????
Rain is falling from the sky
i know it's cause he's crying
And God so am i.
I wanna kiss the Birthday Boy
Where Is My Pride And Joy????
For a happy birthday
Here is where He Should Be!!!!
I Love You Faron Dear
I Love You
Without You Near
There's Only Misery
There's No Sally!!!!
Copyright
on this 14th day in October 2011
send him down from heaven!
(i've been waiting for you
 Faron My Loving Pooh-yours 4ever True)
Sally/S@L whatever you wanna call me

love call of the wild

King Kong escaped from his captor,
going on a rampage.
We were in a fix for sure,
it's unheard of this day and age.
He was just looking for some fun,
when we tried to stop him.
He was loose and on the run,
things looked mighty dim.
And somewhere along the way,
he fell in love with a blonde haired girl.
He only wanted to play,
cause she gave his heart a whirl.
He was more scared of us,
than we were of him believe me.
That's why he made such a fuss,
terrorizing the city.
He was looked upon as a monster,
but to some he was a hero.
Afterall he only wanted to protect her,
from the world that scared him so.
The bigger they are the harder they fall,
and he fell for her like a child.
Yes he was huge and stood mighty tall,
but love tamed this beast from the wild.
If a beast can have a heart,
why can't(all)humans?
When he does wrong instinct plays a big part,
but he doesn't really understand that he sins.
A love affair between animal and human
is not an uncommon thing to occur.
Between beast and man will rarely happen,
because where the wild things are they prefer.
But love should conquer all,
to say the least.
Take a lesson here it's your call,
just know listening w/heart can soothe the savage beast!
Copyright 2010~S@L

LOVEFIGTS ME
FEVERYDAY

the end

NOT

www.ingramcontent.com/pod-product-compliance
Lightning Source LLC
Chambersburg PA
CBHW041534220426
43662CB00002B/53